DEFENDING SCREENS

7 Different Ways to Shut Down a Ball Screen Against Any Player at Any Level

Steven Kaspar

Defending Ball Screens by Steven Kaspar
Published by Steven Kaspar

4987 Warwick Ave
Memphis, TN 38117

http://stevenkaspar.com

© 2018 Steven Kaspar

All rights reserved. No portion of this book may be reproduced in any form without permission from the publisher, except as permitted by U.S. copyright law. For permissions contact:

me@stevenkaspar.com

Introduction	4
Terminology Used	6
One other note	6
Green	7
What it is	7
When to use it	7
How it's done	7
Illustrations	9
Black	13
What it is	13
When to use it	13
How it's done	14
Illustrations	15
Cowboy	20
What it is	20
When to use it	20
How it's done	21
Illustrations	22
Blue	26
What it is	26
When to use it	26
How it's done	27
Illustrations	28
Red	33
What it is	33

When to use it	33
How it's done	33
Illustrations	34
Gold	**39**
What it is	39
When to use it	39
How it's done	39
Illustrations	40
Down	**45**
What it is	45
When to use it	45
How it's done	45
Illustrations	47
Tips for Guarding Ball Screens	**52**
Communication	52
"Good players don't get screened"	52
Mix-n-Match	53
Trust Your Teammate	53
More Resources	**55**

Introduction

The ball screen is becoming more and more popular in the game of basketball at all levels. The point of this book is to give you different ways to defend the ball screen hopefully providing you the ability to shut down any type of player whether that be a dynamic scoring ball handler or a big who can pick and pop and hurt you from deep.

I played basketball for Bucknell University and played on teams that ranked in the top 5 in points allowed against and opponent field goal percentage, went to the NIT twice, and had one NCAA March Madness trip. We used the same defenses I teach in this book and I think they will work for you if implemented right.

In my years at Bucknell, the only way I was able to stay on the floor was to be a great defender and part of that meant being able to defend any ball screen as that was probably 80% of what we had to guard. I think my coaches at Bucknell did an incredible job teaching us various ways and strategies for defending ball screens and hopefully I can teach those and explain them to you in this book.

I will cover 7 different ways to defend a ball screen: Green, Black, Cowboy, Blue, Red, Gold, and Down. They are in no particular order except the couple more common ways are first. I hope they provide you with the tools to stop any ball screen.

Each defense covered has 4 sections

- *What it is* - brief overview of how it will look when executed
- *When to use it* - things to think about when trying to decide which defense will make sense for a certain situation
- *How it's done* - more detailed description of how it will look and things to think about
- *Illustration* - series of pictures that give a step by step visual of each defense

I hope you enjoy!

Terminology Used

As I'm describing the different ball screen defenses I will use the following to refer to the players on the court

- *on-ball defender* is the defender who starts guarding the ball handler
- *ball handler* is the offensive player coming off the ball screen set by the screener
- *screener* is the offensive player setting the screen
- *big defender* is the defensive player who starts guarding the screener

One other note

It might be helpful to look at the *Illustrations* section before reading the *When to use it* and *How it's done* sections to give yourself a mental image of what is being described.

Green

What it is

Green is a common switch. The big defender and on-ball defender switch men and end up guarding each other's man. The nice thing about Green is that it essentially removes any benefits of running a ball screen (assuming no mismatch is created by the switch).

When to use it

Green is good to run when you have an on-ball defender and a big defender who can guard each other's man equally well. Ideally you would be able to run Green with the entire team - 1-5, but you can also run this with 1-4 and use a different defense when the 5 is the big defender. This allows you to switch but not get in a situation where a 5'8" point guard is getting posted up by the other team's center.

How it's done

As the screen is coming the big defender yells "left green - left green - left green" (the context for the direction is found in the Illustrations below). When the on-ball defender hears this, he doesn't necessarily have to move at all he just needs to be ready for the screen and ready to switch.

Just because the on-ball defender hears "green" doesn't mean he can stop focusing on guarding the ball handler. One way to exploit a switch is for the screener to *slip* or *ice* the ball screen after the big defender has gotten above him but before actually setting the screen. This leaves the big defender and the on-ball defender both out guarding one man and the screener open for a quick over the top or bounce pass and a clear lane to the basket.

When the big defender is ready to switch, he yells "switch" and after that the switch is final. Defenses get in trouble when this communication isn't clear - creating even half a second of delay can be the difference in a well executed switch and two guys ending up guarding the same man leaving the other player unguarded.

Now looking specifically at the on-ball defender, there are a couple ways he can make the switch.

The first way is to get underneath the screener. This is a good approach if the ball handler isn't much of a shooting threat and can't just pull up from three as the switch is being made. It also works well if the on-ball defender isn't too much of a liability getting posted up. Since the on-ball defender is running under the screener, he will already be on the backside of the big defender and it will be easier for the screener to dive and pin the on-ball defender on the block and get an easy post entry.

The second way is for the on-ball defender to fight to get and stay on top of the screener. This prevents the quick pocket pass to the diving screener and also allows the on-ball defender to front of the screener if he decides to post up. If the on-ball defender is able to get in front, this will force the ball handler to make a lob entry pass which will be slower and easier to defend since you will probably have some help defense able to break up the lob pass.

The big defender can make any over the top pass hard by providing good pressure on the ball handler after the switch.

Another thing to consider when running Green is how far you need to switch out on the ball handler. If you're switching out onto a great shooter, you need to make sure the big defender is coming out and contesting that shot, but if the ball handler isn't a deep threat maybe he makes that switch from the free throw line and will dare the ball handler to shoot.

Illustrations

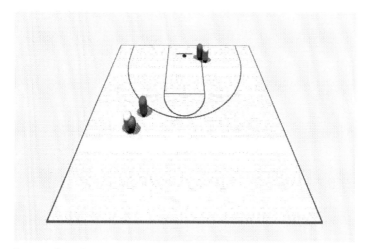

Start of action

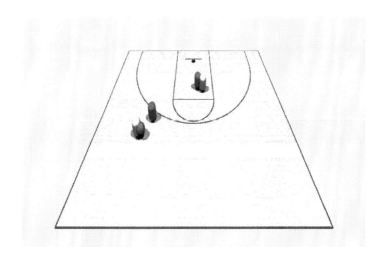

Ball screen is coming

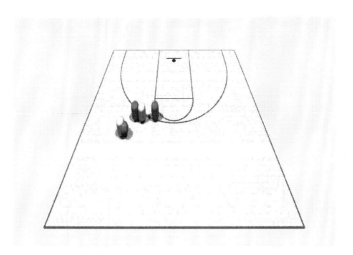

Screener is set and the big defender is ready to guard the ball handler

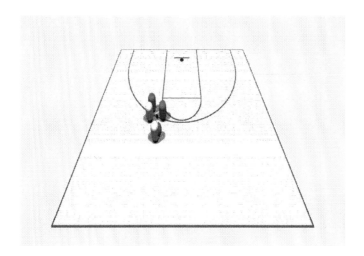

On-ball defender runs underneath the screen. He has the option to go over to help prevent from getting sealed on the block

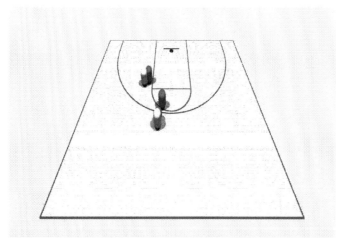

Switch is executed. Now the big defender is on the ball handler

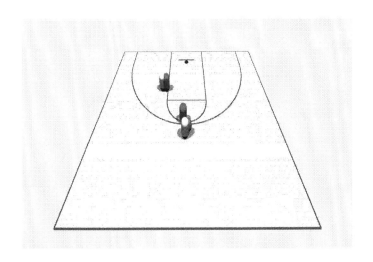

End of the illustration

Black

What it is

The big defender is going to hard hedge forcing the ball handler to go outside of him. The on-ball defender is going to go over or under the screen and under the big defender to get back in front of the ball handler. Once the on-ball defender is passed the big defender, the big defender recovers back to his man with high hands.

When to use it

If the big defender is mobile enough to get out above the screener but you don't want him trying to guard the ball handler, this is a good option because the big defender just needs to get set in the hedge position and be still until the on-ball defender gets back into position.

Black is good to use against an aggressive driving ball handler to slow him down, and is very effective if the screener isn't a big offensive threat. Since the big defender has to get out and hedge it can create a lot of space between him and the screener after the screener dives or pops, so if the screener is capable of making a play from 15' and out it can create some difficulties running Black.

But that doesn't mean Black can't be run if the screener is a threat. It just means that it will require the off-ball help defense to be active in disrupting the screener when he gets the ball and maybe even switching and having the big defender rotate out of the screen to another man.

Black can also be dangerous to run against a good passing ball handler in general because it presents some vulnerabilities with the big defender stepping out that far creating a long recovery. If the ball handler can make a quick pass to the screener, it can create problems and a lot of rotations. This isn't a problem for some defenses that are fine rotating or have good active help defense, but it can be exploited if the off-ball defenders aren't active and talking.

How it's done

As the screen is coming the big defender yells "left black - left black - left black". When the on-ball defender hears this, he needs to shade the ball handler so that the ball handler must accept the screen and cannot reject it to the baseline.

When the screen is about set, the on-ball defender should attach himself to the hip of the ball handler and the big defender should be out extended above the screener creating a sort of wall the ball handler will have to go around.

It is important that the big defender isn't so far out that the ball handler can crossover and split between the big defender and the screener's hip creating an open lane to the rim. The on-ball defender can also prevent this by providing good pressure and staying tight to the ball handler's hip forcing him out around the hedging big defender.

Once the ball handler comes off the screen, the big defender should not move to prevent from fouling (a good ball handler will attack the big defender's hip and if the big defender is moving at all he will get called for a block).

The on-ball defender will go under the big defender to get back in front of the ball handler. Once the on-ball defender has passed the big defender, the big defender should recover back to the screener with high hands.

Similar to attacking Green, a common way to attack a Black defense is to have the screener slip the ball screen early once the big defender has stepped out above his hip.

Illustrations

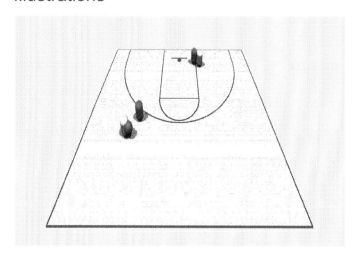

Start of action

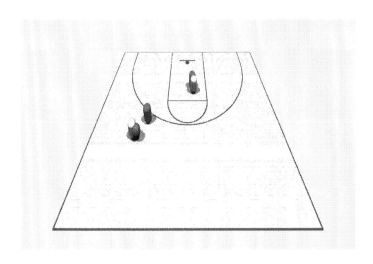

Ball screen is coming

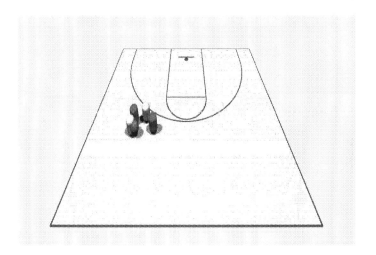

Big defender is out past the screener creating the hedge - he does not move until the on-ball defender has gone under and past him. On-ball defender is tight to the hip of the ball handler trying to fight over the top

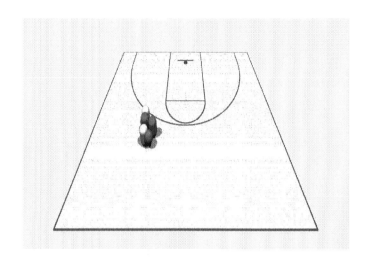

On-ball defender goes over the screen

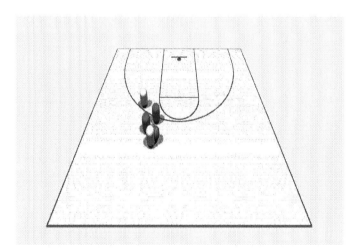

On-ball defender goes under the big defender

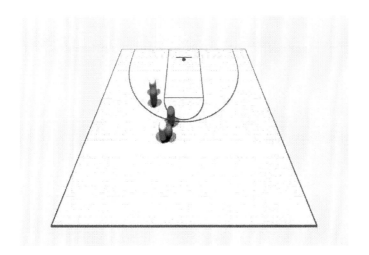

Big defender recovers with high hands once the on-ball defender is past

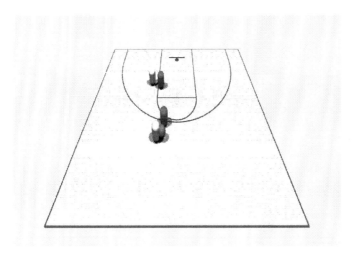

End of action

Cowboy

What it is

Instead of getting out and hedging or getting out to switch, the big defender is going to stay back and wait for the ball handler to come off the screen. The big defender stays there slowing down the ball handler until the on-ball defender can get back in front. The on-ball defender has an option to go over or under the ball screen.

When to use it

Cowboy is good to use when the ball handler isn't much of a threat. If you are playing against a ball handler who can hit a 15' pull-up or can make plays in the paint, then he will be able to pick you apart unless the on-ball defender is a great defender.

When I was at Bucknell and found myself on the scout team, I would get to **pretend** I was an offensive threat so we could practice playing against specific personnel and Cowboy was always my favorite defense to go against because it didn't put very much pressure on me and I could get in the paint and make plays easily.

This can be very effective though if the big defender is a shot blocker and can contest both the ball handler and recover back to the diving screener. It's also very good if you have an on-ball defender who can blow up (go over the ball screen and stay in front of the ball handler) ball screens because he will be back in front of the ball handler allowing the big defender to recover quickly.

Cowboy is also a good fall back option if you are going Black and the big defender can't get out, then you would just fall back into a Cowboy because the on-ball defender will be doing the same thing.

How it's done

As the screen is coming, the big defender yells "left cowboy - left cowboy - left cowboy". When the on-ball defender hears this, he will shade the ball handler so that the ball handler can't reject the ball screen to the baseline. If the on-ball defender is going over the top, he will attach himself to the ball handler's hip or if he is running under then take half a step back and open up to the ball screen.

The on-ball defender needs to be careful about opening up to run under because he will be more likely to allow the ball handler to reject the ball screen and go baseline. Like the other defenses, there is no help from the big defender if the ball handler is able to reject because the big defender is getting to the middle to help.

When the ball handler comes off of the screen, it is very important that the big defender is able to mess with and slow down the ball handler to get him out of a rhythm. If the ball handler knows that the big defender isn't going to provide any help, he will be more confident taking that pull-up from 15' or getting to the rim for a layup.

On the other hand, if the ball handler knows the big defender will come out too far, he can just wait for the diving screener to get below the big defender and make that bounce pass for an easy finish at the rim.

This is why it's so important for the on-ball defender to get back in front of the ball handler, so the big defender doesn't get caught in limbo too long.

I would suggest only running Cowboy if you are confident that the on-ball defender can get over the screen and back in front or if the on-ball defender can run under the screen and you not have to worry about the ball handler pulling up behind the screen for a 3. If the on-ball defender has to run over the screen and can't get back in front of the ball handler quickly then you will have problems.

Illustrations

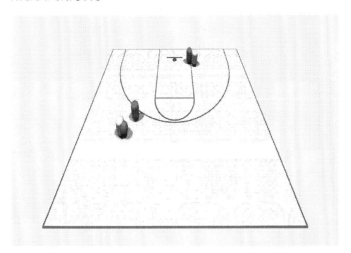

Start of action

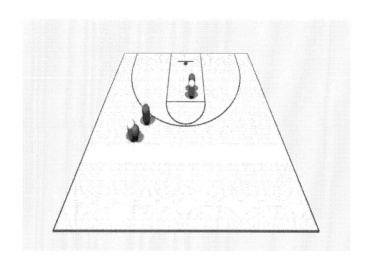

Ball screen is coming

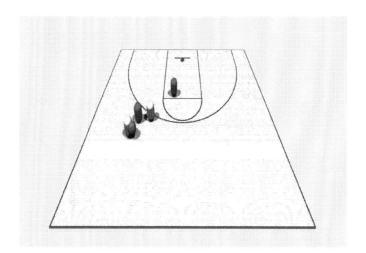

The big defender sits high enough to slow down the ball handler, but not too high that the screener can dive and get below him

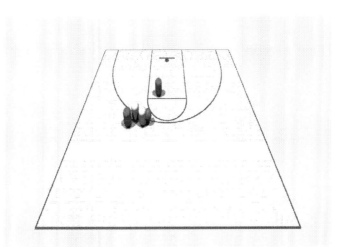

On-ball defender can go over or under, but will probably go over staying tight to the ball handler's hip

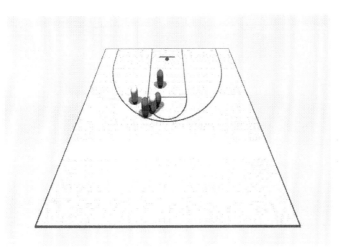

Big defender needs to be active to slow down the ball handler while the on-ball defender tries to get in front

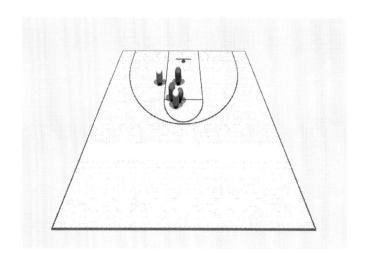

The big defender can't let the diving screener get behind him. That is why it is important that the on-ball defender gets back in front of the ball handler as quickly as possible

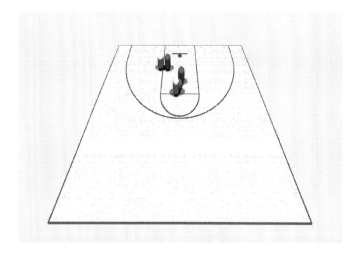

Once the on-ball defender is back in front, the big defender recovers back to the diving screener

Blue

What it is

The big defender is going to come out and be perpendicular to the screener to meet the ball handler immediately when he comes off of the screen. The on-ball defender is going to go over the top and have high hands and good pressure to prevent the ball handler from making an easy throw back pass.

The big defender's goal is to prevent the ball handler from getting to the goal and force him to dribble flat across the court until he picks up his dribble, at which point the big defender can recover back to the screener.

When to use it

This is good to use when the ball handler is a big threat. At Bucknell, this was the defense we would use for guys like CJ McCollum who we just needed to get the ball out of their hands.

Blue is a big commitment because the big defender stays until the ball handler picks up his dribble, so if the ball handler can drag the screen out far enough, it can create a long recovery for the big defender and will most likely require some sort of back-side rotation from off-ball defenders.

When I was at Bucknell (on the scout team pretending to be CJ), this was my least favorite defense to play against because it can be so effective in shutting down the ball handler. It can leave the rest of the defense exposed and force rotations, but this can be a good option if the other team has one guy you need to stop.

How it's done

As the screen is coming the big defender yells "left blue - left blue - left blue". When the on-ball defender hears this, it's important that he shades the ball handler and forces him to use the ball screen. Again, if the ball handler is allowed to reject the screen, there will be no help because the big defender is running out to meet the ball handler when he accepts the screen.

As the screener is getting set the big defender is going to be perpendicular to the screener. This is different from Black where the big defender is hedging out. Here the big defender is positioning himself (1) not get split and (2) to be able to slide with the ball handler preventing him from turning the corner. If your big defender can't stop the ball handler from turning the corner, you can't run this.

In Blue the on-ball defender is not trying to beat the ball handler over like in Cowboy or Black, but he is trying to apply pressure from behind forcing the ball handler out of rhythm and preventing an easy throwback pass to the screener - this is very important - if the ball handler can make a quick, easy pass out of the Blue you will be forced into long rotations.

Now that the ball handler has accepted the screen, the big defender just needs to slide and keep the ball handler from turning the corner or making a quick pass over the top of him. The on-ball defender just needs to stay tight and prevent a quick pass out behind.

This isn't an absolute but it is probably best to have the big defender stay until the ball handler has picked up his dribble.

Illustrations

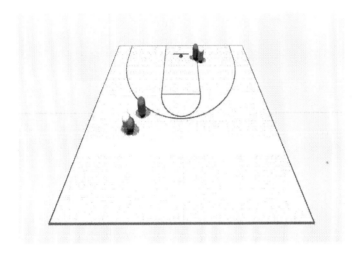

Start of action

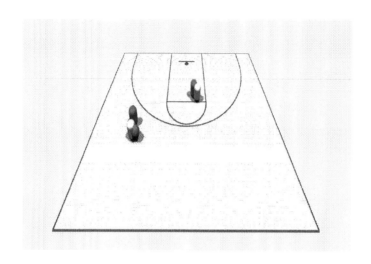

Ball screen is coming

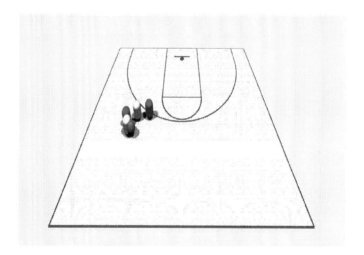

Big defender is perpendicular to the screener ready to guard the ball handler and not allow him to split between him and the screener and also not let the ball handler turn the corner

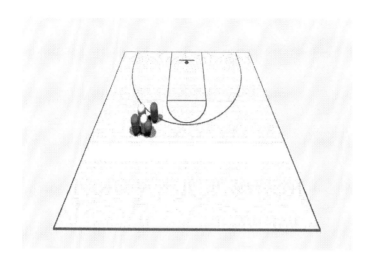

Big defender is not hedging and the on-ball defender goes over the top providing pressure and high hands from behind

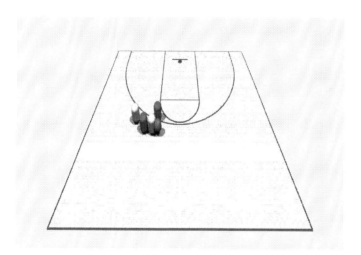

Stay in this position not allowing a quick pass out

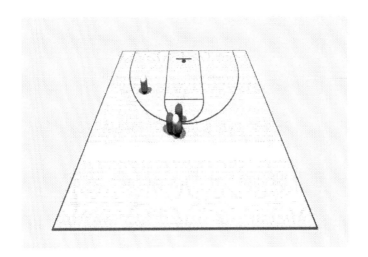

On-ball defender stays behind the ball handler and the big defender stays until the ball handler picks up his dribble

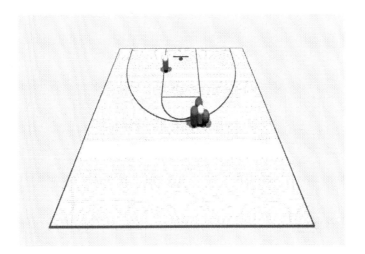

The ball handler picks up dribble, releasing the big defender

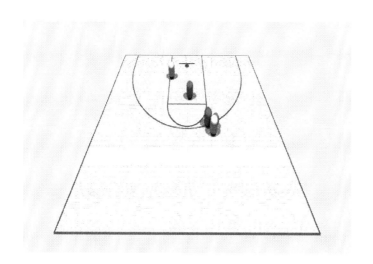

Big defender recovers and the on-ball defender gets back in front of the ball handler

Red

What it is

Red is a more aggressive version of Blue. That isn't to say that if you run Blue on a good player, then you run Red on a great player, but it can be a good change up to be more aggressive if Blue isn't working.

In Red, the big defender is going to be more in a hedge position (almost between a Blue and a Black hard hedge) and is going to aggressively trap the ball handler when he accepts the screen and try to drive the ball handler towards half-court.

When to use it

This should be run under the same criteria as Blue but when you want to try and force more turnovers or just disrupt an offensive player from getting in a rhythm.

It is easier for the ball handler to turn the corner and get to space against Red than it is against a Blue because in Blue you aren't asking the big defender to do as much and extend out as far. This is why running Blue might be a better option to run against a great player even though it is less aggressive than Red.

How it's done

Again, it is done the same way as Blue but instead of the big defender only coming out to be perpendicular to the screener, he is going to be closer to a hard hedge position and force the ball handler to half-court.

Another difference from Blue, is that the big defender should stay until the ball handler has passed the ball out of trap (in Blue the big defender releases when the ball handler picks it up).

Illustrations

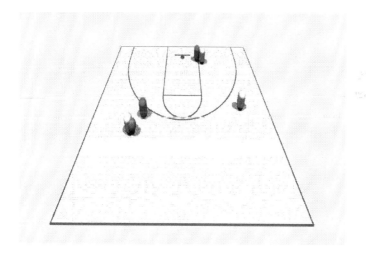

There is an extra offensive player to show how we want the ball to be passed out of the trap

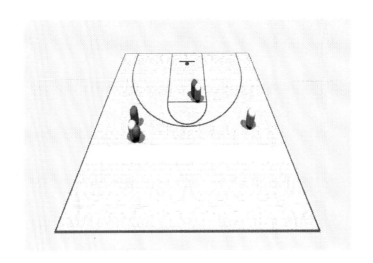

Screen is coming

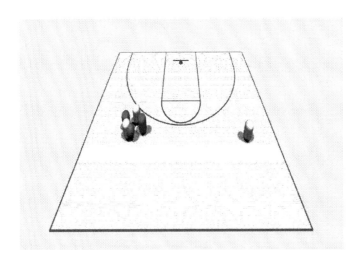

The big defender gets out to aggressively trap the ball handler

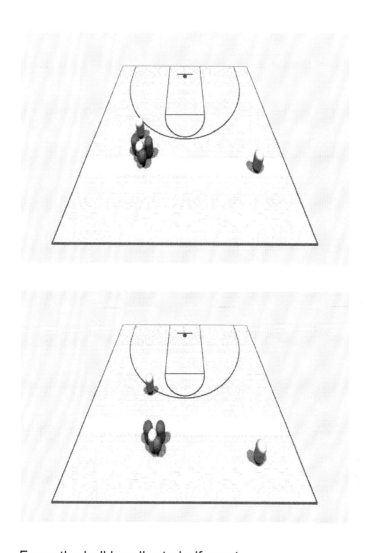

Force the ball handler to half-court

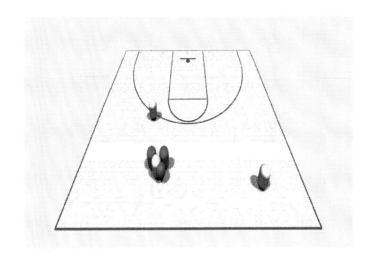

Stay until the ball handler passes the ball out of the trap

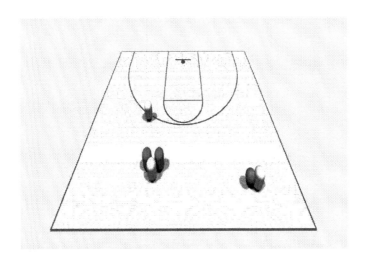

Ball handler passes out of trap

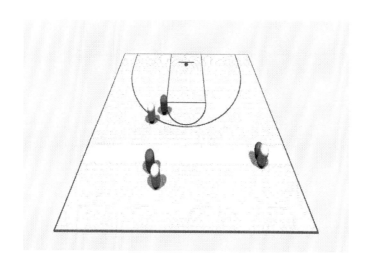

Big defender recovers to screener

Gold

What it is

The big defender stays tight to the screener almost jamming him up and pushing him out as far as he will go. The on-ball defender plays off the ball handler and runs under the screen.

When to use it

Gold is only useful when the big screener is really good and the ball handler is not a threat at all outside of finishing at the rim. Since the on-ball defender gets no help from the big defender, he needs to be able to navigate the ball screen quick enough to prevent a clear path drive, but that is about the only thing you need to worry about if you are running Gold on someone.

How it's done

As the screen is coming, the big defender is going to yell "left gold - left gold - left gold". When the on-ball defender hears this, he is going to release all pressure from the ball handler and make sure that he does not get screened and is able to run clearly under the ball screen.

(If you have a very good on-ball defender, he might apply even more pressure to the ball handler but that is only if you know he can get over the screen and keep the ball handler out of the lane - this won't be the case for most teams.)

Since the only way to get beat on this (assuming we are giving up a pull up jumper) is a clear path layup, the on-ball defender must get through the screen and back in front of the ball handler.

The big defender can help by bumping the screener and making it difficult for the big screener to get good position ideally pushing the screener farther out giving more space to the on-ball defender. Since we are telling the on-ball defender to run under, the higher up we can get the screener the shorter the path the on-ball defender will have to get back in front of the ball handler.

Illustrations

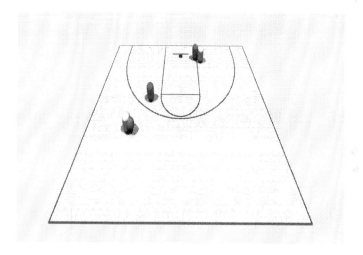

The on-ball defender is already playing off the ball handler since he isn't a threat

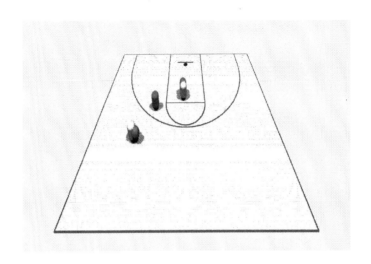

On-ball defender goes even lower when he hears "gold!"

Big defender stays as tight as possible to the body of the screener

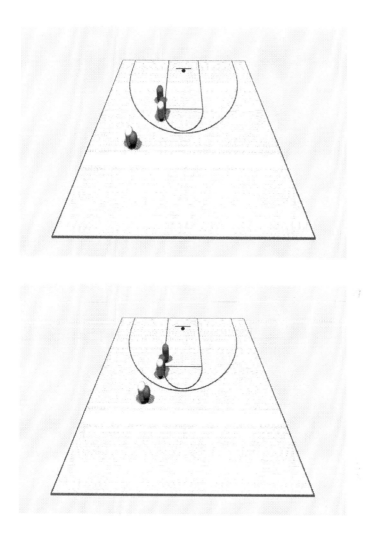

Ball handler can accept or reject the screen

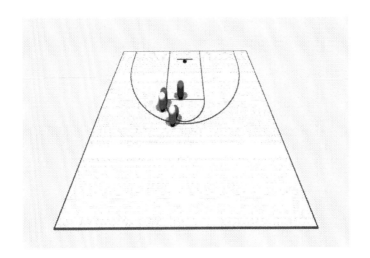

On-ball defender runs underneath and gets back in front of ball handler

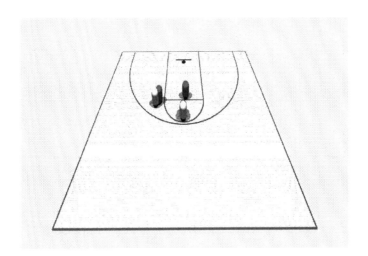

End of action

Down

What it is

The on-ball defender forces the ball handler to the baseline - not allowing the ball handler to get into the middle. The big defender likewise adjusts so that he is ready to help towards the baseline instead of being ready in the middle. The big defender is playing similar to a Cowboy where he is applying only as much pressure as is needed to allow the on-ball defender to get back in position but also not let the diving screener get behind him for a lob and easy layup.

When to use it

If your team forces baseline, this is a great option regardless of the offensive players' strengths. Down is something you will see in the NBA because teams are already forcing baseline so it makes sense to keep the ball out of the middle on ball screens as well.

Down is a great way to really mess up the flow of an offense because it keeps the ball on one side of the court and keeps a dynamic guard from getting to the middle where he can collapse the defense and kick out or score himself if no one helps.

How it's done

As the screen is coming, the big defender yells "down, down, down" - notice this doesn't really require a direction because any screen is just going to be forced to the baseline. If the on-ball defender is already forcing baseline then he should be in position and just needs to make sure the ball handler doesn't get into the middle. If you force middle on the other hand, the on-ball defender will need to adjust to force the ball handler to the baseline. This can be the most difficult part, but if the communication is good it shouldn't be a problem.

Once the on-ball defender has gotten in position to force the ball handler to the baseline, his job is to stay tight to the ball handler's hip so that when the ball handler comes off the screen, he can't easily crossover and get into the middle of the floor.

The big defender's responsibility is similar to Cowboy. He can't get split to the middle and he needs to apply enough pressure to bother the ball handler (this will change based on how good the ball handler is) but not get sucked out too high where he can't also defend the diving screener.

Against a good ball handler, Down will probably require help from off-ball defenders to rotate to the diving screener and allow the big defender to get back or rotate to a new man.

Illustrations

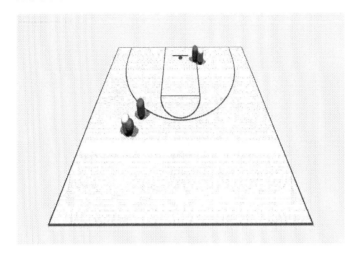

Start of action

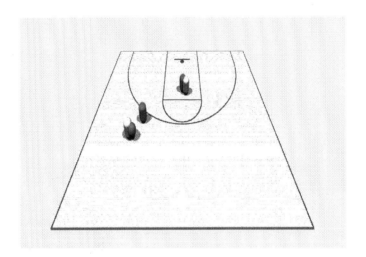

Ball screen is coming

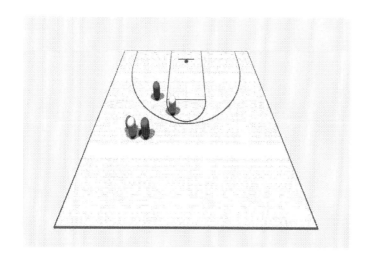

On-ball defender adjusts to force the ball handler to the baseline

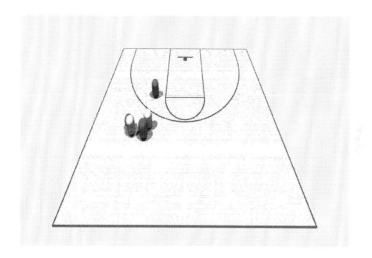

Screener will normally (should) "reshape" the screen to go the other way

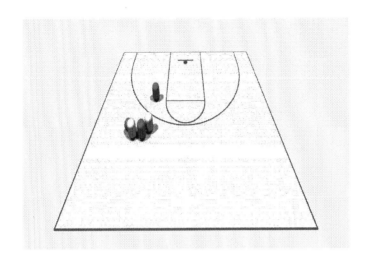

On-ball defender fights over the top to get through the screen

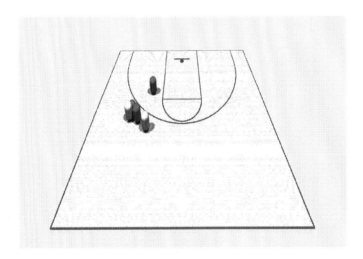

On-ball defender stays tight so that the ball handler can't crossover and get in to the middle

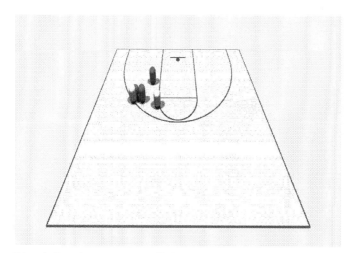

Big defender stays until the on-ball defender is back in position

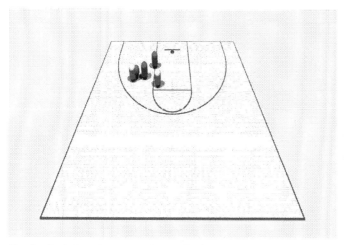

On-ball defender gets back in front of ball handler

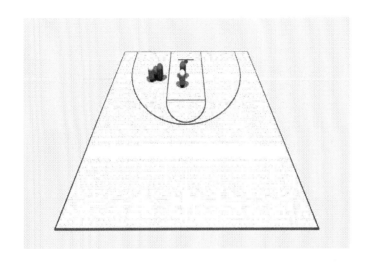

Big defender recovers when the on-ball defender gets back in position

Tips for Guarding Ball Screens

I've learned a lot over the years and have found a some things to be very important and helpful especially when guarding a ball screen

Communication

Hopefully, you noticed the movements in these defenses are triggered by talking. If you don't talk, it doesn't matter what defense you use - it won't work. It is important that coaches emphasize this in practice and that players execute it in the games.

Communication also allows the on-ball defender the most freedom to focus on guarding the ball. If the on-ball defender feels the need to be constantly checking if a screen is coming, he will get beat more often. The big defender needs to talk loud enough and consistently enough that the on-ball defender can trust he will hear and know when a ball screen is coming.

"Good players don't get screened"

This is a quote from my coach at Bucknell, Dave Paulsen - now at George Mason. I don't think it is 100% true (as I think he would concede - a good player will eventually get screened), but it is a good attitude to have as an on-ball defender. Whether you are trying to blow up the screen and go over the top or taking a step back and running under, you will do yourself and the big defender a great service if you're difficult to screen.

One thing I've found very helpful for fighting over the top of screens is to have good contact with the ball handler's hip. If I can keep pressure on the ball handler's hip with my forearm/wrist, I can blow up the screen because I can push the ball handler out (without a foul being called) and get over the top of the screen.

Mix-n-Match

It is common to run different ball screen defenses based on the players involved. Maybe you will run Green 1-4 and Cowboy with the 5. Or run Blue on the other team's best player and Green everyone else. Once you get good at communication and understand all the ways you can use the different defenses, you can use them as needed based on the situation.

Trust Your Teammate

This one might seem odd, but after teaching this to players I've noticed that with the more unfamiliar defenses like Black or Down, players have a hard time really getting to where they need to be because they feel out of position.

For example when running Black, the big defender has to detach himself from his man on his hard hedge to get out far enough to disrupt the ball handler. If the big defender doesn't "trust the process" he won't get out far enough and a couple things will happen (1) he won't slow down the ball handler enough and (2) he won't be high enough for the on-ball defender to go over the screen and under himself as easily.

It's important that everyone knows where they are going and can trust that when they go there their teammate will be in the right position to help and execute the defense.

More Resources

The illustrations in this book are created with a tool that I built and can be found at http://stevenkaspar.com/playmaker. If you would like the playbook of ball screen defenses I used to load into the tool for the pictures, send me an email at me@stevenkaspar.com with subject "Ball Screen Defense Playbook Please" and I will get that to you. It is a free tool for anyone.

I also have a video on YouTube covering these same methods - https://www.youtube.com/watch?v=UQrOdDsulQ8.

You can get in touch by email at me@stevenkaspar.com or on Instagram or LinkedIn or wherever else I have a social media account - I'd love to hear from you.

Please, leave a review with what you thought of the book!

Made in the USA
Coppell, TX
29 August 2021